# (w)holehearted
a collection of poetry and prose

sara bawany

Copyright © 2018 Sara Bawany
Printed in the United States of America

All rights reserved. No part of this publication may be reproduced, redistributed, or transmitted in any form or by any means, including photocopying, recording, or other electronic or mechanical methods, without the prior written permission of the author, except in the case of excerpts embodied in critical reviews, research, other academic or scholarly purposes, and certain other noncommercial uses permitted by copyright law. For permission requests, write to the author at the address below.

Email: bawanysara@gmail.com
Facebook: www.facebook.com/bawanysara
Instagram: www.instagram.com/sara.bawany

Edited by:
Huda Bint Adnan
Instagram: www.instagram.com/hudabintadnan_

Cover Art:
Amina Choudhury
Instagram: www.instagram.com/aminatheartist

Cover Design:
Usama Malik
Instagram: www.instagram.com/40acresphotography

ISBN-10: 1725503670

ISBN-13: 978-1725503670

*dear reader,*

*what you are about to unravel in these pages are some of the most convoluted thoughts that the human mind could possibly come up with, especially one who identifies as muslim, american, pakistani, and female. there are a variety of topics i have spent years writing about, which include femininity, identity, love, heartbreak, colorism, spirituality, family violence, mental health, sin vs. forgiveness, and the like.*

*however, what you will also begin to unravel is an underlying sense of hope and forgiveness. when i began writing initially, it was for my sake alone. i struggled with depression and anxiety for most of my life (along with many sleepless nights), and writing was very much an outlet for me. later on, i realized that my words evoked very strong emotions in others, and thus, the idea for this book was born. there are poems in here dating as far back as eight years prior to today. i was hesitant to include them, but i still chose to because i believe there is something to be said about the deep sadness and yearning of an adolescent. i am grateful that something so painful for me has manifested into a source of healing more powerful than i could have anticipated.*

*i want you to know that although these are my words, it is not necessarily **my** story. much of what i write is metaphorical, and encompasses the painful – and beautiful – narratives of the people around me. please refrain from taking some of these pieces too literally. all i ask is that you approach this book with an open mind and find a space for yourself within these pages.*

*i want my readers to know that they aren't alone in their pain, in their mistakes, and in their heartache. i want my readers to know that there is always light at the end of the long, dark tunnel. lastly, i want my readers to know that it is always okay to ask for help and to be vulnerable. there is so much more shame in destroying the gift that our bodies and souls are than there is in doing everything we can to take care of them.*

*always remember that.*

*with much love,*

*sara bawany*

*my lord, expand for me my chest [with assurance], and ease for me my task, and untie the knot from my tongue, so that they may understand my speech.*

*qur'an 20:25-28*

table of contents:

becoming ...................................................................................7

consuming ................................................................................53

undoing....................................................................................103

repairing..................................................................................163

acknowledgements and thanks.................................................210

ask me
how many times
life broke me
and i will tell you
why
i'm a poet

- thankful

*becoming*

my parents tell me
that i was born screaming
the name of god
i suppose it is a testament
to the *fitrah*
how our deepest instinct
is to find god in all corners
of the earth
and the first breath of air
out of our mother's womb
is no exception

i long to find him again within me
entrenched so deeply in my being
that calling to him is as natural
as it was at birth
but this world
is dragging me
back into the depths of ignorance
and if darkness is where i must
find myself in order to find him
then i pray he
keeps me there

- *fitrah*

dear fathers,
please understand the importance
of holding your daughters
of stroking their hair
calling them beautiful
telling them they will grow up to be
incredible women
hold them
even for five minutes
perhaps the warmth of those five minutes
will save her from a lifetime of hell
searching for you
in the arms of other boys who can
never be a fraction of the man
that you
could have been

- dear absent father

when i can smell
roses and
pistachios
taste the fibers
of mango against
the roof of my mouth
celebrate the vibrance
of all colors of skin
and *shalwar kameez*
hear the gentle clinking
of bangles
on chestnut-colored
wrists
then
i will know
that i
am finally
home

    -   pakistan

all the men
that ever admired me
did so until
i opened
my mouth

- they told me my opinions were too much,
  so i told them i didn't ask for theirs

if you can sit with them in silence
then you will know
the meaning of a soulmate
for the lips
don't need to speak
in order for the hearts
to listen

- true friends know how to sit in silence with you

when i was eleven years old
the lady at the makeup kiosk
proceeded to teach me about
the precise application of eyeshadow
but the first thing she began with was,
"always remember, less is more."
less is more
and just like that
those words stuck with me for the next ten years
and inserted themselves randomly
into various aspects of my life
particularly because
i used to be afraid of writing short poems
because flowy colorful diction
came more naturally to me
and it seemed to me
*that* was the only way to write
but it is now i understand that
less is more

- short poetry

the audacity
to assume
that as a person of color
i will step off the sidewalk
to make space
for you

as if your ancestors haven't
plowed through us
shoved us aside
sliced our egos to pieces
enough times

- sidewalk battles

my psychologist remarked many years ago
that i was like a forty-year-old trapped
in a sixteen-year-old body
my *imam* doesn't know what to say
when i cry my heart out in his office
my therapist told me yesterday
that i am a challenge to counsel
and that he always
has to be on his toes around me

i am not sure what any of this means
because if i leave the experts speechless
and if the people who are supposed to be
neutral and just tell me what is wrong
are so damn intrigued by the depth of my pain
how then, does anyone throw me out
into this ocean of vulnerability
and expect me to float?

- the anomaly | the problem

nostalgia
after diving into another story
from the scent of musty pages
and crisp careful ink
these highlights of others' lives
are woven so intricately to hurt
in all the wrong places
but to minimize pain
in all the right ways

- the easiest way to manage your pain is to become engrossed in another's | why books were my most faithful companions as a child

r un. you have spent your whole life doing so. from failure. from anything that could jeopardize your false sense of perfection. even from yourself.

a sk the difficult questions you were never allowed to. *what is your purpose? what were you created for? is this all there is? why do we suffer?*

m editate on these questions. let them fill you up and consume every fiber of your being. bow your head in *sujood* and seek guidance.

a llow your creator to speak to you. learn from his book. learn about his book. read the signs around you. enjoy the beauty of the little things.

d raw your own conclusions. use the intellect you were blessed with. you are allowed to question. never let anyone tell you otherwise.

a nswer. because while you may question, it is also your duty to seek answers. this is why you are here. this is why your existence matters.

n urture the knowledge and let it grow. cultivate your *iman.* allow it to blossom. remember that you, young soul, were made for paradise. find it. seek it. live it.

- recipe for *ramadan*

so i guess i will spend my life swinging
on this bridge while never being able to
fully step on either side
and i will grasp the rails made of holiday lights
and *daaghas* and in both take pride
and i really do think that the bridge is okay
because you can stand from above
and smile at both lands
with loafers on your feet
and *churriya* trailing down your hands
you never have a home
you can never fully call one place home
but isn't there a beauty
in walking two worlds alone?

- sentiments from the children
  of immigrant parents

/ an excerpt from tedx speedway plaza, march 2016

as a woman
it takes everything in me
not to apologize to a man
for my emotions
i will have to spend the rest of my life
unlearning the way i have been conditioned
to feel
like a burden
like a leaky faucet

no more excuses
for my natural disposition
or for my ability
to swing between
passion and rationality
do not tell me i am too emotional
for i
am not the one who started
all the world's wars

- woman

eight years plus several badly concluded therapy sessions later and his hands shake as he stirs his coffee. i study him. i wonder if my curiosity and apprehension can be mirrored in his posture or if the years have made me forget that he always looks tense. his eyes dart back and forth around the cafe but, well, he was always the walking embodiment of paranoia. as for myself, the fear has never quite left even though i have now blossomed into a woman. i have been the same height for eleven years but i remember him being taller. by god, he was so much more intimidating when i was a little girl. i would seek some type of normalcy from him but it was always out of my reach. his kindness came with a price. his love came with ultimatums. anger flowed from him like a raging river. but now. now his eyes don't frighten me the way they once did. i no longer flinch when he raises his hands. the unprecedented anger has left his eyes and has been replaced by exhaustion but i, i still think of pain and social anxiety and solitude when i think of my father. i know this world has not been gentle to him. but if only his few good fortunes had made him softer. perhaps his hands wouldn't tremble with anxiety as they now do. perhaps the gray hairs would have made their appearance much later. perhaps he wouldn't feel like a stranger to his own children.

- meeting #11

your inability
to acknowledge
entire
civilizations
and experiences
beyond your
white picket fence
does not make us
"exotic"

- fetish

blind love is causing your soul to rot
yet you still fail to conncct the dots
i'm begging, i'm pleading, why can't you see?
he will never allow your peace to be
pierce the darkness with morning light
let its clarity overcome your sight
in the fleeting moments
it's your last breath he compromises
the sun sets as your soul now rises

- please don't die a slave to him

/ a desperate, unfinished, unsent poem to mamma, age 17

she spends what should be a childhood
discovering the affliction of womanhood
then bears the pain of pregnancy
then bears the agony of childbirth

a man can't even bear to be in
the same room to watch this
unfold but then he calls us
the weaker sex

    -   irony

there has been a dead bird lying flattened in defeat on the corner of university avenue and 21st street. eighteen days have gone by and i wonder how many people pass it by wondering how it died, thinking "someone should really clean that up" but it won't be them tonight, whereas i, wonder why i haven't been the one to do so. as a species of higher thought, how can we stoop so low that we seem to lose our respect for human life, quick to take a knife to others' throats and quicker to run away when we find the high road and our loved ones don't. our brothers and sisters in this world are dying horrible deaths but all we can talk about is how the oppressor is being oppressed. spare me your explanations as i save myself from this generation where kindness needs determination so unheard of in this "great" nation. lost in ourselves, lost in these vanities, we shut our ears out to any form of tragedy. this world is losing color but we have always been blind and the ones we trust penetrate our morals to change our mind and if for one second we decide to look up and care, the people around us drag us back to ignorance and despair. everyone keeps saying we are in the greatest age this world has ever seen but the homeless people on the corner of guadalupe street would say otherwise because they're the only ones who don't live in disguise. the rest of us plug our ears with headphones, busy our eyes with cell phones, shut reality out with silicone, and then we wonder why we feel so alone. in a way we are all that dead bird on the street corner, lost and lonely with priorities out of order. and i wonder if, maybe if, it had gotten another shot at life, would it still end up falling prey to this world, ignored by passerby, maybe, i wonder, would it have survived?

- bystander

so much
of our energy
is spent on trying to
please people
while
ironically
people
are our greatest
source
of
suffering

- growing pains

sunday mornings are different. they are for re-evaluation and gratitude. for watching the sun rise and scatter hues of lavender and pink across the atmosphere, making you wish you were witness to it more often. they are for getting in your car with the windows rolled down at 7:38 am and perusing the same streets you do every morning, the difference being that the world is a little quieter than usual.
on sunday mornings, silence is tolerable, welcomed even. it is composed of a few precious hours in which we have the opportunity to take a break from the hustle of life, the grind of a 9 to 5, and the fast-paced activities that leave very little room to smile at the sky and be thankful for a sunday morning where we can do just that.

- soulful sundays

my (single) mother
paints the house
installs two light fixtures
gets the toilet to work again
laughs and tells me,
"what else can we do
if all the men in our lives
turned out to be useless?"
but then
when i work long hours to
make a living for myself
she asks me why
i work like a man

    -    internalized

i wish i was the kind of girl
with a fiery temper and quick mouth
the kind that can snap back the fastest
smartest retort to those who try to
step on her toes
and put her identity in boxes
but even after all these years
after all the times i've been wronged
people's cruelty and hypocrisy
still manage to
stun me into silence
every
single
time
and i hate myself for being hopeful
that next time it won't happen
that friends
and loved ones
and older people
deserve at least seventy chances
to prove themselves wrong
but it happens again
and once more
i say
nothing

- fear of confrontation

and at the end of the worst days
that have been riddled with self-doubt,
the setting sun reminds us that even
the most terrible endings can be beautiful

- *maghrib*

to watch eagerly from glass windows
and feel the vibrations of
melodious *qur'an* recitation
through these walls against which i lean
but not be able to stand shoulder to shoulder
with my sisters in prayer
and touch my forehead
to the ground for eternity
alongside them
this
is the ultimate test
of *ramadan*

- seven days

i hold my breath as i prepare to send a text
my mother warns me i will be disappointed
but i am a little too optimistic
"what's the worst he can say? no?"
i type, "can you help me with my loans
and rent for this month?"
i am struggling
with anxiety in my chest every morning
i don't know what it's like to live a life
where worrying about money isn't
the first thing on my mind when i wake up
he responds with sarcasm,
"i have $50k in old credit card debt plus
$11k in medical bills
can you pay my debt?"
oh
i'm sorry that the divorce with mamma
which you refused to give her
cost you eight years
several thousand dollars
and three children
sorry i forgot that your insistence on how
you provided us with money
(but not with love)
was your biggest argument in court
for how great of a parent you were
sorry i never once asked you for anything
all throughout these years
even though as your daughter
it is my right
(and you are an engineer)
but thank you
for reminding me that pretending
you are my father again
will always be a mistake

- absent father | the root of all my problems

her eyes are bloodshot from grief
we sit there in silence and
after what seems like hours
without looking at me
she finally speaks,
"it was such a great injustice on you
at such a young age
to have known the pain and tribulations
of your mother,
was it not?"
i look at her square in the eye and say,
"i think a bigger injustice would have been
if you had those pains and tribulations
but no one to listen to them."

- my mother will always feel like she wronged me, but i will forever be indebted to her for teaching me how to listen

## (w)holehearted

*after nayyirah waheed*

give me the hardness
the excessive valor
the scared and insecure boy beneath
locked away for years
all the fragments of yourself that your father
and his father
and his father before him
taught you to hide
to make you stone-cold and acceptable
to someone else's standards
of what a man should be
i will shatter the hardness into a million pieces
and from the remains
nurse back to life the flowers that
once secretly bloomed within
the ones you left parched and thirsty
the ones you neglected for so long
while you let them die
did you remember
that half of you is made up
of your tender mother?

- hyper-masculinity

there is always one out there who we all know
who faced such calamities, suffered blow after blow
here, i cautiously weave the story of one
who has the ability to light up a heart like the sun
masked and hidden over the years
covered up by the constant shedding of tears
pain and hurt and pain again
with no one to turn to, and no true friend
and she bore the marks, heavy on her heart
but ever did she strive to play her part

what causes human nature to accept the worst?
when we get two strikes and can't bear a third?
what caused her to settle for less than the best?
when her life's been nothing but a long grueling test?
how could she have let someone take her power?
who gave him the right to make her bow down and cower?

there were no answers; nothing was straight
it went in circles; it was her fate
right and left, people stereotyped labels
but she lay her faith down on the table
like cards waiting to be snatched away
yet ever patient she remained
no one had an understanding of her pain
how her losses were always someone else's gain
they criticized every move she made
and when she cried for help, there came no aid

and through all these years, they can't help but ask
what did she live for, what goal, what task?
where did she get the courage to stay?
because she loved them too much to run away?
was she doing it for herself, or was it society she pleased?
was it herself or the norm she tried to appease?

life must have treated her so damn bad
that she turned to the eight-year-old child she had
to tell the truth for once, to pour it all out
to be able to tell someone what the lies were about

to relieve maybe a small ounce of stress
and make a steady effort not to digress
back down the path of darkness and submission
an appeal for its permanent abolition
and ever so gently, life took its course
for her choices and actions, she has no remorse

why did she stay so long? why didn't she go?
does anyone save herself truly know?
did they legitimately try to comprehend?
did they reach out to her, extend a genuine hand?
did they cry with her when she cried with them?
took her for granted, and called themselves a friend?

took three steps forward, and they put her back two
put the pieces together without any glue
and a time came when enough was enough
an opportunity for freedom, a game played rough
but how was this courage to miraculously appear?
to save herself from drowning in misery and fear?
taking chances in a world plagued by chaos and craze
she emerged into sunlight, completely unfazed
no one could stop her, for god was surely on her side
now it was her own rules by which she'd abide

- her chosen path

to be able to
choose
between the lesser
of two evils
is a
privilege
always remember that

- elections

children crying, the oppressed are dying
yet we worry about which celebrity's lying
it's our carelessness, it's our gossip,
and our heedlessness that will destroy us all
a lack of more intelligent conversations
is the trigger that will result in our fall

- wake up

it was 1999 and the image
of my little brother receiving a heavy beating
still burns in the back of my mind
in all his four-year old innocence
he had replied, "mamma"
when you jokingly asked him for the millionth time
who he would marry when he grew up

what the hell did you think you were doing
asking your son about marriage
from the day he was born
and then expecting him not to be hyper-sexualized
an innocent child, or both?

how insecure a man do you have to be
to fear your four-year-old son stealing your wife
that his answer
so commonly found among innocent toddlers
struck a nerve with you
what else did you expect him to say?

the only woman he had ever known and loved
was his mother
and you dared to ask him to think of another this way
at the tender age of four?

shame on you

- one of many memories that can't escape my mind

the night is
too quiet
and my mind is
too loud
to bear it any longer

- insomnia

she drowns herself in creams
and turmeric
has dreams
of being tall and pale
the kind of woman that all men
and their mothers desire
but she doesn't fit the bill
the mirror
has become a place of self-loathing
and it awaits her arrival
every morning
she stares at her reflection
wills herself to disappear
as if to say
with skin that color
she should never
have existed in the first place

- (un)fair and still lovely

## (w)holehearted

at the heart of every conflict is injustice
and rarely in the history of the world do you not see war
breaking out over it
silence is not a vocabulary word when it comes to the battlefield
tell me the last time everyone you know turned the other cheek
when a racist tweet was posted
when your least favorite celebrity appropriated my culture
when another black body joined the ever-growing list of deaths
at the hands of the police
our system may be broken but our war cries are not
yet, when the battle is even closer to home
when the battleground is our own bodies
when our livers and our spleens and our hearts and our brains
are cannibalizing each other
each starving for their right to live
why do we stay silent?
when suicide becomes an option
when our fears are dismissed as childish
when antidepressants are forced down our throats
and then down our kitchen sinks in shame
why do we not speak up?
they say we have about three hundred bones in our bodies at birth
but they mesh together to form two hundred and six
as we grow older
i think it's funny that our bodies put more effort
into holding themselves together than our minds do
they say that when one human being suffers
the whole world is at loss
when you are struggling to maintain your sanity, make no mistake
you may be a dent in the world, but your pain is forming craters
in this body we call humanity
make no mistake, you are at war with yourself
make no mistake, you are a raging battle
you are a war zone in disguise
do not be afraid to weaponize yourself, to raise the white flag
to ask for help
god gifted us these bodies as an *amaanah*
do not forget that they will speak against us one day

- home front

we teach ourselves to
hide our hurt behind waves of anger
learn to mask our sorrows
behind alcohol or chocolate
maybe pills
sometimes all three
transform our tears into sweat
building all the muscles in our body
simultaneously allowing
the most important ones
(our hearts)
to shrink
and this is how
we begin to lose
our humanness

- suppressed

strange is this life
the greater the number of people
that claim to know and love you,
the lonelier you are

    -   the fame complex

women are not your teddy bears to be
poked, prodded, chewed up, and frayed
we are not your second choice
your last resort
your backup plan
or your favorite sport
we are a set of ideas
things of beauty
and creative minds
that have trained themselves to maneuver the cruelty
and be cunning in a world which is
not made for woman kind
we bear you in our wombs for nine months
only for you to tell us that we are beneath you
because we came from your ribs
we are not inferior to you
you
are a part
of us

- on being a woman

"i always go for the skinny ones,"
he says, waving the statement about carelessly
"my ex? 95 pounds. the other one? 92 pounds."
because i don't know what else to say
i just shake my head and laugh
but inside
my 103-pound self is burning with shame
and self-loathing
was i just
never
good
enough?

    -   body image

early on, we grew accustomed to sharpening our ears for the sound of his footsteps and immediately put away whatever we were doing so as not to be faced with his unforgiving glare. the list of words we were never allowed to say grew with each passing day, including words such as "love" and "dad." my little sister told us many years later that she would force herself not to cry because that would only make him beat her harder and my younger brother learned the word "terrorist" at school and began to refer to my father as one. all the while, my mother was never allowed to speak one word in our defense because doing so would only make matters worse.

- inside the belly of the beast

close the door behind you
contemplate the world one last time
shut the blinds, you're not alone
welcome to this daily horror of mine

turn yourself around to the chaos
as a new environment unfolds
but let no one else suspect a thing
the room grows more and more cold

close your ears so tight
no, please keep them exposed
for there is more yet to hear
these emotional verbal blows

turn around, thrown in all directions
the arguments and yelling never end
a moment of peace, perhaps an hour
is all i ask of you to send

close-minded, narrow train of thought
the same cycle, building on itself
years upon years of trauma
stop, please just comply for once

turn the opposite direction
unsurprisingly there are new battles
everywhere, it's just everywhere
hands wring, brain rattled

close your eyes, step outside
a breath of fresh air, the sunset's vivid hue
smile, laugh, and pretend like it's all okay
and it really is because it's behind you

turn. turn where? where is there to go?
gradually losing sense of this entity
what i once used to call a family
has now become an enemy

    -   spectator

the unfathomable pain
of the mother
who has lost her son
to the cruelty of human selfishness
haunts the hearts of all
who meet her
as they feel her tears against their cheeks
as they embrace her quivering frame

even when she smiles
the sadness doesn't leave
it has made itself
a permanent home in her eyes

- naila's grief

/ in memory of ammar tariq, 12/19/1990 - 04/17/2016

despite what society
has tried to hammer
into my mind
everything
i have learned and seen
tells me
to fear the white man's voice
over
the black man's body

- #blm

the other day, my *khala* comes into my room and tells me that rehana is here to see me. i have no knowledge of who this is so i ask her. she explains to me that rehana is the maid that she had several years ago who took care of me as a child the last time i was in pakistan. i wait and she walks in. fits the profile of every maid i've ever encountered with the difference being the huge loving smile on her face. it is infectious. i warmly embrace her and she sits at my feet. i get upset, and tell her to please sit next to me on the bed but she refuses. we talk. she lives a three-hour bus ride away and came just to see me. she worked for my *khala* for eight years. now she is a mother. she has five children. she asks about my life in america. about my siblings. tells me how she used to feed me a bottle every night to make me sleep. i wish she would sit on the bed with me. she used to tell my *khala* to let her know next time i visited so that she could come see me. here i am, seventeen years later. i look so much older. i grew up so fast. i ask about her children. i wish she would sit on the bed with me. i am tempted to move to the floor where she is. but if any of my relatives walk in, i will never hear the end of it. that i reduced myself so low. that i wrinkled my nice new clothes. i don't understand the point of wearing such clothes if i have to constantly worry about creasing them. i wish again and again that i had the courage to get to her level. i don't.

and several hours later, my passive acceptance of this class difference still eats at me. because i know what i actually think. i know what the prophet would have done. i know that i dislike the vast difference of status here. i know that i cringe every time my relatives ring a bell meant to call the servants because i can't imagine anything more demeaning. even though i know they pay them better than most others do. i notice how everyone that works here is very dark-skinned. overlooked. some are sharp-mouthed. some are kind. can't do anything right. but we still need them for the job. and that's all they are. working class. subhuman. but we still need them for the job. poor. diseased. but we still need them for the job. but we still need them for the job. but we still need them for the job.

something about long walks
they have a habit of making people fall in love

*consuming*

i imagine that
poets
must be the best
kind
of lovers
they can take
a mangled body
and turn it
into
magic

- poets heal others in more ways than one | if only they could heal themselves this easily

tears always form in my eyes
every time i think of how
i never learned how to cry
because i used to pride myself
as a child
for never resorting to tears
now as a woman i thank
my body for slowly
teaching itself how to feel

    -   evolving

i am on a
never-ending drive
to self-destruction
but the wildflowers guiding me
on the side of the highway
remind me that there is still
beauty
on this road
to hell

- wild

the first time he tells you he loves you
it is appropriate to laugh
ask him if he's ever known the feeling
of a thousand supernovas colliding
and let him know what his heart is in for
ask him if he has learned the art of sifting
through the stardust
that broken women leave behind when they try to heal
when he tells you he loves you
but doesn't speak with his hands and lips what he does
with his tongue
then keep an eye out
for even comets in danger of hitting the earth
sometimes barely swerve and miss
only to return years later
when he tells you that you are the one for him
ask him if he is ready
to hold the solar system in one palm
and all the galaxies your eyes contain in the other
and still let you lead the way
ask him to count the black holes
that your heart has left behind
and promise not to add to them
when he says he loves you
ask him if he is able to watch you bloom in all your glory
without vying for the position of the sun
ask him what he can offer you
that the rest of this world
can not

- a universe of promises

i don't want your sympathy
your condolences
your donations that will pay for the coffin
where she buries her sadness
you have been blind to her tears
and deaf to her cries for help
don't come back now with your thoughts and prayers
don't kid yourself into believing your presence here matters
how dare you look me in the eye when i tell you this
how dare you raise your chin
as if you ever did a damn thing for her
as if you didn't walk by her in the hallways
as if you didn't overlook her
every time she opened her mouth to speak
as if you didn't exclude her and only her
from every circle you created
as if she ever found a home with the people
the universe told her she was supposed to belong to
as if home was so easy
as if home isn't now six feet deep and lonely
as if home wasn't even lonelier than that

- the funeral sermon

the warmth
she never found
in you
she now seeks in
other men

tell me
what kind of a love
is that?

- what father's day?

i gave my chastity away last summer, that beautiful august night when we succumbed to our demons and released all fears of the consequences. i remember the feel of your hands on my bare legs, caressing them under my white skirt as your lips met mine for the very first time. my heart was chirping that night in tune to the crickets around us as we sat in that courtyard, while you held me close as i'd never been held before.

i gave my chastity away that night as you picked up my body and carried me down the steps, into your room, onto your bed and suddenly, the lust that i never knew existed inside of me made its appearance. it was our first time but somehow the rhythm of our bodies synced in tune as if they'd meant to join together all our lives. it was all we could do to not take all our clothes off as the smell of your sweet skin filled my lungs and your fingers combed through my long curly hair.

i gave my chastity away and i didn't care, for the peace i'd been searching for all my life, i found in your arms. our bodies entangled, your heartbeat matching mine and your kisses sending sparks down my spine and i finally understood what all the great poets and writers spoke about since the beginning of time. it was the happiest night of my life, as we explored each other's bodies until the sun began to rise and then prayed the morning prayer together as if we hadn't just committed a grave sin. but when you lay your head in my lap and looked at me with those soulful eyes, everything faded away and nothing mattered as much as you and i.

- the beginning (of the end)

cast me not a second look or a hello
carelessly continue on
with your life
walking purposefully looking straight ahead
like a horse with blinders
ignoring
outstretched arms wanting friendship
or just your presence
finally notice me
as an obligation or a body or a means to an end or
a way to make you feel good about yourself
but
as much as i would die to be in your company
i will not feed your ego
you can stay isolated with your few
and i will find myself among those who
don't have to try too hard
just to remember
that i
am still
here

- i am not an afterthought

depression is that friend you never wanted, it's that feeling you're being haunted. you tell yourself to snap out of it but the prospect of smiling again is daunting. it's a boulder in your gut that inspires self-hatred and it's taunting you. it eats away at your liver every time you try to recover and tears form in the corners of your eyes because things haven't been alright for a while. the prospect of eating is absurd. of cleaning or showering, it's unheard of. it's a virus, it's a disease, you don't know what but you want it gone. carve deep cuts into your chest begging your soul to rid itself of this unwanted guest, catatonia takes its place and eventually there is nothing left. it's a pit of endless gloom, and your heart it will consume, tunneling your body for its own room, the companion you never needed with you.

- a coming of age

/ an excerpt from amplify u.t., april 2017

(w)holehearted

there is nothing more
intimate
than his head resting
against your chest
listening
to
your heartbeat
and when he says,
"hear that?
it belongs
to me."

- forever

for someone
to love your body in one night
more than you have loved it
your whole life
can instantly turn intimacy
into self-love

- body image pt. iii

nothing
nothing
nothing
has the power to bring one
to tears more than
the sound of pain
in another human's voice

- empathy

you, fresh cut and carefully trimmed beard
with your thirty-one hashtags while on your fourth beer
you, spend your saturday afternoons in the back of a hookah lounge
and your friday nights in the corner of the
loudest club you found
you, pornography loving, feminist hating
claim to be the nice but misunderstood one
who will come along and save her
from all the other boys before her who were just
like
you
ask fatima for a picture without her *hijab* while
commenting under mariam's photos for her
lack of *hijab*
i, can sniff out men like you from miles away
your cheap cologne isn't enough to suffocate
anyone who has heard you lecture women about how they
shouldn't be wearing perfume
and you, reek of double standards
and i am tired of watching
your mother break her back
to save the reputation of your sorry ass
while the very women you destroy
are considered outcasts
who fall into the trap
and promises of forever
because they believed that maybe this time
a man could actually be telling the truth

to your mothers, i'd like to say:
1. if our tradition has taught us that men are supposed to "take care" of women, why have you taught them to do everything except that?
2. if our prophet wouldn't defend his wife aisha when she was accused of adultery until god himself sent down the truth, what makes you think you have the right to defend your son's outrageous behavior?
3. if you're going to teach your daughters that the honor of the family falls on their shoulders, then at the very least teach them not to marry sons like yours

and to them i'd like to say,
even if you can keep your internet history clean
for more than just a few hours
you still don't have the authority to lecture me about
the purity of my heart
got the nicest watch on your wrist
but you've been caught red-handed
with those signature catch phrases
that escape your lips so candidly
*insha'allahs* and *masha'allahs* scattered through
every other sentence
your religious persona may be believable
but the good stuff's in your dm's
this poem is not an apology
i am not sorry for your discomfort
i see you squirming in your chair
and the phrase "not all men" on your lips and i
am the furthest thing from interested
this, is a eulogy to your facade of masculinity
because i just burned your ego to the ground
you better take off that plastic crown
because when my sisters
still receive unsolicited pictures
from men they will be standing behind for *isha*
in just a few hours
i assume
exposure just isn't a problem for you
and full disclosure
you bet every disgusting message you have ever sent
that you
are just exhibit number one
we have built a museum of your secrets
and your reputation is about to be undone

- an ode to the muslim fuckboy

just because
virginity
manifests itself
physically
in a woman
does not mean that
virginity
only
belongs
to a woman

- chastity's double standards

come fly with me, don't run away
arise and shine with the light of a new day
remove the blindfold from your eyes
let's both stop dealing with these lies
the value of patience pays well in the end
so maybe it's best to keep our heads turned and pretend
and the tomorrow we want is the one we'll wait for
let's make that promise, and i'll forever be yours

- empty spaces

sometimes, the way i love you makes me angry. rips me apart. drives me mad with rage over my choice to desire someone so difficult. my mother asks me why of all people i had to pick you, but i have asked myself this question for years. my best friend tells me she has seen me taking the hard route repeatedly, and i suppose she has a point. i have never made things easy for myself, and choosing to love you is no exception. i always find myself gravitating toward the road less walked, and all the years we have cried and fought have taught me how to run. we are in a better place, but that place indicates distance, and distance indicates separation, and separation leads to agitation and i am not sure how much more of this i can handle. i go back and think about all the choices i made and all the opportunities i turned down because i was convinced that it was nobody but you, you, you, that you were the one for me. and despite everything to come, and regardless of the time i will ache for you to be by my side again, it is not in my capacity to stop believing. i have always loved challenges, and such is fate that i have now fallen in love with one. as painful as it is, nothing else could feel more right.

curling up against your body like it
was a wall gave me the protection
against the rest of the world
i never knew i needed

- storm shelter

i raise my eyes to the starry heavens
helplessness flowing to their brim
overlooking this valley which stretches to such lengths
that my blurry vision can't comprehend
your name rises to my lips
and guilt surfaces simultaneously
because i
should have tried a little harder to save you
for your self-destruction has carved a path sharply
through these dunes beneath my feet
but alas the overlap of our two worlds ends too soon
and i am forced to stand on the edge of this cliff and
helplessly watch
because you, my friend, walk a fine line
between salvation and darkness
and how i wish i could hold your hand
and lead you to the right side
part the sea for you to walk through
be your moral guide
but heroes
are not born, they are burned
over and over
and they rise from their ashes with hot coals in their eyes
and a fire in their heart
creating a trail of embers to lead themselves
out of the dark
how i pray and hope, my dear friend
that you can find your own light
to not succumb to the dark and to shine your brightest
because you
deserve so much more than
what you settle for
and i am grateful for our time
but i must learn to accept
that you
must rebirth yourself
you
must be your own savior now

- phoenix

bliss
is when
he pulls you onto his lap
rests your head on
his left shoulder
and whispers,
"welcome home."

- home is wherever you are

one year ago
he was singing
*kabhi khushi kabhie gham*
barefoot
while folding his dress shirts
and his socks

and it was in that moment
i knew
that
he
was
the
one

his contentment and the ease
with which he walked his chosen journey
was something i wanted to wake up to
every day
for the rest of my life
because his was a path
i would never tire of walking

- insignificant moments turned extraordinary

beat me down, go on and berate me
take me down, keep on tormenting me
gone is the terror that would escalate
when your tongue was snickering at my fate
you fake fools thirst for more blood
as my water-less eyes continue to flood
over and over and over and over
lips ache for more and more news to savor
gone are all my weakened days
i'd waste away in continuous dismay
but despite the sky being a misty gray
i stepped out one day and found my way
what a heavy price i was obliged to pay
for the wretched choices that i made
through this ocean of pain i wade
gone is the vitality which continues to fade
i don't need you to sympathize or apologize
because these eyes have seen real lies
you ask about all the what's and why's
and i say it's time i claimed my prize
thumbs up to those who keep it real
not belittle others to get over how they feel
i'm not asking for your approval or fame
i'm just fed up with all these games
no one forced you to like who i am
and frankly, i don't give a damn
but learn to keep that mouth of yours closed
for would you like your weaknesses exposed?
know that you will never understand my life
the struggles i've fought, my perils and strife
just like i will always be baffled by you
and at your inability to state what's true

- because words kill | high school angst

i need you
to kiss
all the uncertainties
off of my tongue

- your lips are the cure to my anxiety

it is the biggest insult
to be purposely left out
of your narrative
as if i was never responsible
for so much of your success
you were no match
for my ability to spend sleepless nights
taking all your broken bits
and fashioning them into gold
but i am sorry i was still
never good enough
you see, i was simultaneously trying to
mend the glass shards of my own sanity
which you conveniently dismissed as selfish
i am sorry that my honesty about my pain
was worth nothing more than you
telling every listening ear about
how i never made enough time for you
when time was all i gave you
even when i had none left
to give myself

- hourglass

leaving was the second most
difficult decision i've ever made

the first was coming back to you

- the cycle

poetry flows like streams with all the sights we see
when we hear the rustle of the wind on branches
and the taste of our insecurities' ashes
the embrace of burning skin against your beloved
the way white sheets feel at 3 a.m.
yet we lack appreciation of smells and scents
so allow me to honor them
mother's apple pie on a warm november night
brings back fond memories of better days
pollution rampant in kunming, china
rubs your nostrils just the wrong way
the smell of cherry blossoms by the river
signals the coming of a blooming spring
ambrosia smells of evanescence
while the aroma of chocolate makes your heart sing
miami shores smell of salt and brine
and the ships that never made it home
dirt reminds you of the countless graveyards
where you buried your ancestors' bones
your hair smells of fresh apples
but your skin smells barely alive
turmeric reminds you of the motherland
while the stench of failure keeps you up at night
grass smells of freedom
when commencing into texas back roads
so give yourself up to the world of fragrances
and discover new abodes

- aromatherapy

you put walls up
but leave doors open
you give them the key
to shake your foundations
to the core
and then wonder why
they destroy you

- the disconnect

## (w)holehearted

some people spend their whole lives
never knowing the feel of passion
of fire in their souls
the kind of love that drives them mad with desire

everyone
should know an all-consuming love
at least once in their lifetime
so that when they find a peaceful one
they can appreciate its serenity

    -   the love that swallows you whole will spit you right back out

the thing i miss about him the most
is the way he would kiss my hands
brush his lips across my wrists
caress each knuckle and
trace the lines on my palms and fingers
as if to say that every little part of me
was worth loving

people spend lifetimes trying to understand
what it means to love themselves
but he taught me how
in minutes

- what love taught me

he doesn't know it
but she is there with him
every night
she feels his fingertips tracing her curves
her lips caressing his spine
and she slips in between his arms to feel his warm touch
one more time
begs his eyes to embrace her the way they used to
tousles his hair while he sleeps
maps his face into her memory with her palms
and this is how she misses him

- fantasy

my confidence doesn't come back
but my exes always do

- the cycle pt. ii

having sex
is different
from
making love
one
uses your
body
while the other
reveres
your soul

    -    hookup culture

the meadows are green
everything appears serene
each water droplet gleams
a beautiful image only in dreams

there are smiles on our faces
so happy we can almost taste it
but walk afar a couple of paces
and something dark leaves its traces

between the hopes for dreams coming true
though over time, the love in our hearts grew
something underlying appears so shrewd
a hesitancy, a fear so crude

and suddenly my image of you shatters
remakes itself behind the plaster
everything feels as if it's a disaster
and my pounding heart begins to beat faster

wandering in doubt, lost in thought
through the battles and struggles you've fought
it's the just and rightfulness you've always sought
but through it all, it's been me you've never forgot

take hold of this branch and climb with me
higher and higher atop this lifeless tree
let's revitalize it and set our souls free
i'm begging you to believe in a you and me

    -   a love undefined

people tell me that i have better options but
i'd rather spend the rest of my short life
being wildly happy and reckless with you

- and ever

and when she wears your necklace
around her neck
she remembers your hands
around it too

    -   violence is not a form of love

## (w)holehearted

it is 8:08 a.m.
rent is due in 11 days
i have been at work for 8 minutes
and there is already sweat on my brow
i am calculating how many more hours i
need to sit at this desk
how many more rich white folk i need to
drive around this city
to their tasteless and expensive bars
just so i can pay my rent
which is due in 11 days

about 36 feet away from my desk
two sorority girls are banging adamantly
on the closed doors of starbucks
devoid of their morning caffeine and sugar
which is worth an entire hour of my paycheck
and while i panic
about my rent being due in 11 days
i wonder
how strange it is to
share this world
with millions of people
yet be a universe apart

- what middle class?

leave me pressed between the pages
of your favorite book like
just some other exotic thing
unfold me like your favorite flower
that has just ripened for spring
frisk the petals of my self-confidence
off one by one
bury my roots so deep in the ground
that even i have to search to find them
this is how to destroy me

- and how i entrust you not to

they say it takes twenty-one days to break a bad habit but it has been three months and my hands know exactly what to do when they find yours. i am stuck in a perpetual cycle of resisting the urge to intertwine my limbs with yours and showing up at your door all the same. i tell myself this can't last, i can't stay long, someone will know, someone will see, that god is watching and he will punish us eternally. tell me how am i supposed to set fire to this and burn it all down when i have been alight from the very first time you held my hand. when our love has been burning holes in my skin. in my lungs. and in my soul. tell me how am i supposed to let you go when i have come to love the flames. when i have created a home out of this fire.

- in love with the way it burns

my depression returns to me like an ex that can't take a hint
when saying "no" to the heart making its way up my esophagus
isn't enough for it to leave
it brings back all the bad habits i pushed away
reminding me why i worked so hard to cleanse myself of it
in the first place
i could argue that it's like an addiction
but i never really wanted it much to begin with

my depression has a mind of its own
on the days i feel liberated from self-hatred
it will peek its head through the door of my office
which i decorated so carefully in confidence and say hello
for the thirty-eighth time
as if this isn't the fortieth time i have begged it to go away
when it tries to convince me yet again of the reasons for its return
(i'm not finding a job, i made a mistake at my job,
someone i thought was a friend turned out not to be, it's tuesday)
it tells me things are different this time
tries to convince me why this toxic relationship is so good for me
reminds me how much i have come to rely on the sadness
as if i don't have enough voices in my head
as if each part of me hasn't already waged war on itself
tearing my very existence apart
it promises me it will keep me company on those sleepless nights
so eventually
my walls break down
i stop putting up this fight

my depression has carved a home for itself in my chest
an overstayed visitor, an unwelcome guest
sometimes it brings its side piece anxiety
but i know my depression's only ever had eyes for me
words too
tells me how much god doesn't want me
how much the world doesn't want me
even convinces me how much i don't want me
encases me in the four walls of my own self-hatred
and claims to be the roof

and when i get fed up
when i have cried my eyes out to capacity
when the sunshine that used to radiate from my smile
is gone yet again
i finally stand up and tell depression,
"you are wrong
god has spoken to me in avenues
that you have yet to walk through
i am capable of love and of being loved
by everything other than you
i worked hard and i deserve to be where i am
this is the last straw
i am finally taking a stand."

but like every abusive entity
it throws back its head and laughs
puts an arm around me like i am some silly little child
reminds me it is always here with the ghost of a smile
and in that moment i force myself to walk out
of the home i have slowly turned into my own grave
to do all the things i don't want to
to go see that friend i have been neglecting
to pick up the phone and call my father
i swallow my fear
and force it back down my esophagus
in the pit of my stomach where it belongs
where i pray it stays
and as it leaves i am warned of its return
of its whispers that tell me i am nothing without it
that it is a part of me and i can never escape
this might all be true but
for the dreaded question of
if there's more to this life
i am convinced there is one without this sadness
and for that i will keep searching

- conversations with my depression

there's an obscure path i've begun to trek
internally, i am an emotional wreck
i wear a smile to disguise the shame
again and again, it's myself i blame

numbness suffocates my sense of sanity
my past haunts me, selfishness turns to vanity
i hear my heartbeat in my ears
a young soul that has aged a million years

evil thoughts run through my head
words i wish i could have said
my dark side threatens to win this war
i forget what purpose i am living for

never felt so abandoned and afraid
through my own blood i swim and wade
time as i know it slows before my eyes
but i know i am not yet worthy to die

emotions masked while life goes on
failure to see hope in a new dawn
this chasm in my heart grows wider
i think i have ceased to be a fighter

- downward spiral

the burden of being
the only thing
between
options
and suicide
. . .

- the gray area | the last resort | the phone call

i have been stowing away false promises
and broken sleep cycles
in between my teeth
i suppose that is why i have been grinding them lately
stress has found a home for itself in my neck
but it has been migrating toward my jaw lately
i find myself unknowingly clenching my lips together
as if to refrain from bursting out
with all the things i want to scream
to expose all the wrongs
the secrets i am forced to carry lately
i suppose
the older i get, the farther the pain
makes its way into the recesses of my mind
because it is so much harder
to massage a jaw than it is a back
so there is a sense of permanence
to this bitterness lately
and i do not like the way it tastes

- routines

i want to believe that god
created your lips from the leftover dust of stars
that you came into existence and the cosmos
held its breath for just a minute
and the planets whispered to each other
that this one
was different
because how else would it be possible
for shooting stars to erupt in my heart
every time your fingers touch my cheek
and for the earth to tremble
when you raise your hands in prayer
only the light of your being
could cause the sun to go blind in jealousy
and induce entire galaxies to crumble
every time you say
'i love you.'

- transcendent

long hot showers
unspeakable sins
the dark side
quick fiery rage toward the people i love the most
abused but also a spectator
used but also power hungry
temper one second
tears another
an extremist in every way possible
from one side of the pendulum to the other
periods are straight from hell
nice boys that call me beautiful must therefore
be from heaven

middle grounds never existed in my book
until i turned nineteen

my worldview shifted to accommodate many lenses
i learned that islam comes in many different flavors
that not all people are simply good or bad
just lost
or found
i learned that categories are tricky
and putting people into boxes ends in lots of confusion
and soggy cardboard
i learned that high heat on a hair straightener
is never a good idea but low heat on the stove
will not cook your scrambled eggs
exactly the way you like them
i learned that life is a jungle of both effortless and
backbreaking paths
that oceans can be both menacing and welcoming
and most importantly
i learned that there are three sides to every story

- balance

(w)holehearted

i didn't know
it was possible
to spend a lifetime losing
the same person
over and over
but here i am
and there you aren't

- the cycle pt. iii

i am preparing my body
for a war in which
both winning and losing
will break me

- discipline | difficult decisions

(w)holehearted

*undoing*

stained
marks of sin lay invisible on my skin
which only my fingertips recognize
tears fall and pool into my pores
as i set out for another day in disguise

touched
broken
like a cracked egg
like an old crumbling tower
like a book with its pages ripped out
stripped of all its power

contaminated
while showering
i scrub my skin raw
yet the invisible scars remain
i suppose i am destined to keep going
head held high
heart drowning in shame

tainted
i walk this world with a scarlet letter
that only i can see
but it is enough for the self-loathing
to embrace the deepest parts of me

tarnished
i laid bare every crevice of my body
in hopes that someone would love my soul
now i have embraced the marks
for never again could i be whole

- impurities

i've watched love bring
grown men to tears
and to their knees
turn them into
little boys
and strip them of all their pride
i have witnessed men
cry in the laps of women
on their shoulders
broken-hearted
broken
while confessing their
deepest fears
placing all their faith
in the hands of women
so do not for one second tell me
that god designed
men to not feel a thing
that god made men
"better"
than women

- hyper-masculinity ii

if my body is ever found at the bottom of a pond
with my *hijab* floating on the surface
i pray that this brutality is never reduced to a random crime
if my body is ever found in my apartment
with bullet holes in my *hijab*-wrapped skull
i pray you never have the audacity to call it a parking dispute
if my body is found lifeless in an abandoned house
in the bad part of town
i pray the rest of the world never turns the other cheek
and accuses me of dealing drugs
says that maybe i had it coming
that maybe i was in the wrong place at the wrong time
as if there's a right time to die
that maybe i asked for it
that maybe i shouldn't have been out at night
when i should be able to walk home without having to
fight for my life
that maybe
just maybe
islamophobia and hate crimes had nothing to do with it
but if the roles were reversed
they'd be calling me the terrorist
see, isn't it just funny how the media insists
on zooming in on the beard of every radical extremist
that blows up another building in the name of isis
but won't even publicly announce the name of the "clean shaven"
white man in a white van that ran over muslims leaving a mosque
you see, hatred in this world has always been contingent on
who's doing the perpetrating
if i attack, it's terrorism
but if i'm attacked, it's just another assault
and sentences are dependent
on the color of the perpetrator's skin
as if the darker it is
the faster you think in question marks
a litmus test
the lighter you are
the lighter the verdict
as if white men didn't destroy entire civilizations
and don't continue to do so

have the coroner who inspects the remains
dissect how dangerous a young muslim girl
possibly could have been to the monster of a man
who felt the need to end her life so effortlessly
believe us when we tell you there is a problem
that muslims everywhere are reminded that we have to hide
that this world was never meant for us no matter how much we try
that the america we breathe and live and aspire to change
will chew us up and spit us out
*hijab,* beard, medical degree and all
see, isn't it just funny that white supremacists
will target a new community every few years
so long as they don't look like them or believe in what they do
while they conveniently erase from history books
that jesus was a dark-skinned palestinian man
see, isn't it just ridiculous that elementary school curriculums
teach us about the holocaust each year
but tell black people to stop bringing up slavery because it's divisive
tell bosnian and rohingyan muslims to shut up about their genocides
tell palestinians it was never their land in the first place
because it doesn't fit their narrative
and isn't that all we have ever been?
just something to fit their narrative
imagine being so devoid of humanity
you have to strip someone else of theirs just to feel alive
just to maintain your privilege
this is the plight we find our world in
but do not for one second think we will
close our eyes to your monstrosity
that we will come break bread with you
to talk about how you can make our oppression a little easier
and when my body hits the ground in prayer
that you do not reduce my death to an accident
i will make sure my fall is heard around the world
because god
god doesn't choose martyrs by accident

- death wish

the ones
with melancholy embedded in their eyes
that no amount of laughter
can disguise

you know the type

- trauma

what is hidden and perceived dead
will always find its way back to life
for darkness is nothing
but the absence of light

when adobe walls and lined green carpets
begin to feel like
dipping your toes into cold water
hold your breath as you go deeper
murmur all your preparatory prayers
your eyes will dart side to side
let them
this building felt like home once
or its alter ego in another city did
i can't remember
aren't they all houses of god?
now, it is a battlefield of its own
you slide into water that boasts purity
but reeks of salt
and judgment
waist deep now
you try to find solace
in the group prayers but you can't stop
formulating poems in your head about fear
hands clenched, body tense
as unfamiliar faces contribute to the
claustrophobia settling in
how can safety be conditional?
aren't you supposed to feel safe and at home
with the people you call brothers and sisters?
but your brothers and sisters
can't stop telling you that
your views are too radical
your art is too political
your poetry is too whimsical
your makeup is too noticeable
but god
god made you beautiful
and you only remember that as soon as you
step out of these walls
and sometimes you have trouble
remembering at all
but for now
take a deep breath
step over the threshold

your head goes under
the cold water numbs you from words
that are thrown at you like knives
as you still search for acceptance in these depths
but drowning repeatedly in cold shame
that is handed to you on a silver platter
should teach you
never to make a home out of ice water
shouldn't it?

- for a religious community's scapegoats, outsiders, and rejects

we meet again at the same breakfast joint from many months ago. his hands still shake as he pours eight creamers into his coffee. it is the first time i can remember having a conversation with him that isn't riddled by discomfort. i do not feel forced to look down or away as frequently and my smile feels natural, for once. i have reached a milestone in my life and even though my father doesn't say it, he is proud of me. he is concerned about how far i drive and he reminds me of how he drove 88 miles to work ten years ago to provide for us. 88 miles. that's the exact number i drive now to get to and from my own job. it's funny how things come full circle. how we promise ourselves we will never be anything like our fathers, yet here we are. and their remnants live on in us. like the fact that it took us both only two and a half seconds to mentally calculate the tip. and how we both can inhale ice cream by the gallon. and how, as much as i hate to admit it, i inherited my quick temper from him. but i feel at peace with our relationship for the first time in my life. i pay for our meal and he says 'thank you.' the words sound foreign coming from his mouth. he even looks taken aback by them. and this is just one of many things that have changed in the last few years. and if my father has learned how to say 'thank you' and 'i love you,' then i know this change won't be the last of them.

- meeting #14

people express
amazement
that cruel words can have
such a massive effect
on others
yet
they forget
that one mosquito
has the power to massacre
an entire nation

    -   the worst kind of pain

my body oscillates like a pendulum
"balance" is a word foreign to its vocabulary
but it knows "stress," "pain," and "betrayal"
it is still trying to learn the word "cry"
when the anxiety hits, i lose full control
my eyes can twitch for sixty-eight days straight
i can go to all the therapy in the world
i can write poems until my fingers bleed
but my hair will continue to separate itself
from my scalp by the handfuls
so my body still betrays me
and i don't know how to convince it not to

i fight by seeking out long-forgotten pleasures
i watch the sun rise in the mornings
even though i know i will be left staring
at the darkness above my bed at night
i work my body out until i can't feel
the difference between the pain in my legs
and the pain in my soul
and tomorrow i won't get up
not because i can't but because i
just
can't
i have learned
that there are some fights that can not be fully won
but i have promised
that i sure as hell will keep trying

- balance pt. ii

and i know now that
your loving me
healed the parts of me
that were broken
but my loving you
shattered the rest of them

- you still couldn't save me | but thank you for trying

old photos haunt me now
i am only in my early twenties
and baby pictures shouldn't make me cry
but they do
and photos from high school
shouldn't make me wince
but i can't help myself
i don't recognize the me in them

my face has thinned out over the years
people used to call me pretty but now
the hollow in my cheeks
is the kind of contour that makeup could never carve
forms the kind of holes that years of disappointments
dump their tears into

so then
what do i make of myself now?
who is this face staring back in the mirror?
who did i think i was to shed so much of my skin
so that i could be all colors of shame and sin
so that i could finally learn how to feel
something?

- growing up is overrated

those who
never ask for much
are the ones
who usually need
the most

- hidden | having needs is what makes us human

i didn't want to come home today
my empty room, dim lights
because i would finally have to face it
the guilt
me and my sins
trapped in my room together
i couldn't bring myself to shut out the chilly night wind
but i closed the door and the air stifled me
i was overcome with fear and sadness and longing
as i collapsed onto my prayer mat
and the guilt began to release itself
through my eyes and my nose
through my ragged sobs and the nerves
which wouldn't stop trembling
for the addictions we develop are not so easily overcome
"but dear *allah*," i pleaded
"your mercy is so much greater than my sins
and if you forgive me this once
i promise never to do it again."
i was fifty-three days clean and holding my own
but i succumbed once again and my guilt
chills me to the bone
if the loneliness i face in this life is my punishment
then let it take the place of the fire of your hell
for i have spent my short life yearning to please you
and be near you
but i strayed so far away
and i am having trouble finding my way
home

- addictions

you always say i deserve better
but you refuse to let me have it

- selfish

i should have known from
the moment your mother felt
the need to thank me for being your
friend that there would come a day
when i wouldn't be

- red flags

we deserve
the kind of
love
that brings us
to
our
knees
in gratitude

- *shukr*

tensely listen to the tick of the clock
hearts everywhere mold into rock
in the depths, a key slowly turns the lock
everyone says it's someone else's fault

the wind blows viciously outside
there are no more rules by which to abide
every so often, someone turns the tide
precious moments of laughter never last long

everywhere i turn, i discover a lie
somewhere far off, someone sounds a cry
a plea, a desperation, a hopeless sigh
picking up after those that stir up trouble

how much more can anyone take?
which straw will be the last to break?
how many more smiles shall be perceived as fake?
vacuous souls evince their true states

these falsehoods we build with walls around
blocking out external truth and sound
a lie or commitment by which we are bound
changing the rhythms of the waves

when is this cycle going to end?
how many more friendships will break and then mend?
for the last of the rules which we maliciously bend
finger-pointing arises everywhere

these thoughts eat away at my head
with words that i blatantly should have said
and the signs i ignored, which i should have read
endless trust issues cycle again

it's time to make my presence known
among all those fighting for the throne
the threads of life so delicately sewn
define the morality of this race

harmony comes crashing down
reality takes on a meaning newfound
head in my hands, i block out the sound
but i will never cease to believe

- mistrust

to have your worldview
shattered

that
is the ultimate
heartbreak

- lens

say to all the
conservative, traditional
parents out there
that there are much worse
things in this world
than your daughter
marrying
a man
she
loves

- "love marriages"

the sadness lives in my throat like a parasite
i feel the lump every time i swallow and
no amount of smiles can make it hurt less
on days when it becomes too much to carry
it moves into my chest
gnawing at my ribs
where i threaten to tear it out
along with the rest of my heart
towards the middle of the day
it makes its way into my arms
finding a home for itself in between
my shoulder blades and in the crevices of my neck
so now i know why my shoulders slump
and why sitting straight hurts
in all the places it shouldn't
and on other days
i feel it clawing its way through my stomach
destroying the pieces i've so carefully rebuilt
and through tears
i laugh at those who tell me
that emotional pain doesn't manifest physically
because every day
my heart stops and clenches in on itself
as if to punish me for breaking yours

- heartbreak takes two years on average to heal from
  but no one tells you how long it takes to heal from
  being the cause of it | maybe we don't deserve to know

stop
apologizing
to the man who sees
your naked body for the first time
for your breasts being too small
or your shoulders being too wide
for the hair on your arms or
on the back of your neck
because
you, my dear
are a work of art
fashioned by god himself
and that man should make it
his life's work
to love your naked body
to treasure your naked soul

    -   body image ii

woman, remember
it is not your job
to help him discover
what he wants
chances are
that even at the end
it still won't
be
you

and what a gamble it is:
allowing the very person
who broke your heart
to mend it for you without
promising to stay

- paradox

men
like
you
need
their
egos
shattered

    -    and their bones

and what a shame it is
to feel like
a stranger
amongst the very people
whom you call
home

- exclusion

it is 11:43 pm on the night of halloween
and i am still at work typing away
i am supposed to go to a gathering afterwards
these are the only thoughts on my mind
my phone begins to ring and i am surprised
my mother has never called me this late
i pick up cheerfully and in just one minute
the entire night has turned around
she says, "he's been in a car accident
the police found him having a seizure
even long after his car was lodged
headfirst into a tree on the side of the road."
i haven't talked to him in months
i can't stand to be around him for
more than two minutes to be exact
but in that moment i feel panic welling up
at the bottom of my throat
"he's going to be okay," she says
i hang up and tears spring to my eyes
it seems i have forgotten how to breathe
and at 11:46 pm
four minutes before my shift ends
i find myself in the middle of a fit of hysterics
pressing my palms over my mouth to muffle
the incessant urge i feel to scream and scream
it is at this moment that i discover the love for him
that i never knew existed inside me
when i realize that there is indeed a difference
between liking someone and loving them
tonight i also learn that blood ties
can never truly be severed
many years later i probably
still won't be able to tolerate him for
a little over two minutes
but right now
i just ask god to give him
a little more time

- this love was not an accident

marry a man who kisses your feet
and looks at you with full moons in his eyes
wears his heart on his sleeve only for you to carry
gets excited at the little things
remembers what you want to name your children

    -    regrets

you can have the best weekend of your life and it doesn't matter. seventeen people will have told you how beautiful you look. your eyeliner wing will turn out right on the first try. you will smile and laugh with friends and take beautiful pictures, setting aside two-hundred and twenty-five of the best ones in an album labelled "the perfect weekend" to prove that you should be happy. but let me tell you. it doesn't matter. because at 6:58 pm on a cold october sunday when the sun sets and the day ends is the beginning of the gloom. you will not sleep that night. you will scroll through those two-hundred and twenty-five pictures and not recognize yourself. midnight is a great time to let the tears begin. you will read very raw poetry that will shatter the few pieces you put back together over the last few days and the tears will flow harder. you will feel ungrateful for not praying the extra two *sunnah* during *isha* because you were so tired. but here you are three hours later with tears falling down your pockmarked cheeks and not knowing why you can't just escape into slumber. this is what depression looks like. you can experience immense joy for the first time in days, but end the night hating yourself without understanding why. the heartache resurfaces as if you need more reasons to cry. you will tell yourself repeatedly about how many things you don't deserve, and yet, how lucky you are to have them. the words people praised you with which made you glow with pride will stab at you like knives when nightfall comes. this is the beginning of the end. and when you finally escape into sleep and wake up the next morning, you will hardly remember. you will go on about your day. you will smile, you will work, and you will wait. because depression is a disease that never fully goes away. and the impostor syndrome that comes with it will be the final reminder that even happiness is an achievement you were never meant to obtain.

i always thought that
being in love was supposed to
lessen the pain
but for me, it only escalates
what does this tell me about
the way i love?

- toxic

my self-respect
must be buried so deep within me
if every man i encounter
believes he can
repeatedly
cross his boundaries
and believes
in his darkest of hearts
that i will forgive him
each time

- when he doesn't understand the
 meaning of 'no' | but it's not my fault

# (w)holehearted

*after joss whedon and rupi kaur*

i have a slight obsession with skylines, bodies of water, and quiet nights. skylines remind me how small i am in this world. how, if nothing i do matters, then all that matters is what i do. bodies of water remind me of god's grace and beauty. how water is soft enough to offer life, but tough enough to drown it away. how water is life. earthly life. and if i don't tread carefully, life will wash me away too. quiet nights remind me of the darkness i once occupied, and where i may find myself once again if i don't stay carefully balanced between the luxuries of this world and the permanence of the next. so essentially, these things i revere, i've also come to fear. because too much of a good thing can be bad, and too much of a grounding can make us forget to look up sometimes. to remember where we come from, to remind ourselves of the bigger picture and the grand scheme of things, is so important. and it's why i write. why i seek to mold words and thoughts into something others can reinterpret according to their own experiences. pretty words and thoughts, though seemingly trivial, are what help me get through these days, one at a time. and i am forever grateful for them. *alhamdulillah.*

how ridiculous that upon your entrance
into my home
my first instinct is to grab my *hijab*
and cover up from you
protect myself from your gaze
and your tongue
as if the blood on your hands isn't mine
and the blood in my hands isn't yours
how ridiculous that even after all these years
my amygdala fires a little too rapidly
when you're around
that despite my childhood
being full of memories of us
you are still unfamiliar and foreign
to the most instinctual parts of me
how ridiculous that your name on my tongue
has long since lost meaning
but that my name on yours
brings back fear

- how ridiculous that we try so hard to make trauma disappear but it never fully dies

arrogance gets the best of us
when we say to ourselves after
losing a friend, "we don't need them anyways
god will put someone better in our lives."
have we ever thought that maybe
it's the other way around?
that perhaps god took us away from them
because we were bad for them?
that perhaps he will bless them with
someone better because *we* were not worthy
of their company?
were they a punishment or a test?
or better question: were we?

- misconceptions

sticks and stones may break my bones, but words will always hurt the most. casual remarks stab like knives, and mere sentences can destroy lives. the difference between a yes and no, the difference between a do and don't. do we take into account small words like these that can cost a life? do we ever take a moment to reflect on the people that our lies affect?
shackles, chains, the whole damn game. drenched in falsities down to my name. try turning back but it will never be the same. hold the arrow, i'll take aim. let the dust settle, let them meddle, let them come closer so i can finally strike. hear me for the first time, breathe for the last time, our eyes meet, but understanding is left behind. tell me, in your life of sin, do you really think you'll ever win?
scorch in my gaze, defiance in yours, and you will never make sense of the damage until there's no time left. win or lose but you end up with bruises. nosebleeds, concussions and you grow more confused. when will your all ever be enough and when will your time ever be worth theirs? how much can we take before we break and how much more shall we strive to please?
look into their eyes and find the scars unseen by those who refuse to listen or care; it's a traumatic experience and slowly tears start to form. step into their shoes for a second and maybe, just maybe, you begin to realize. cry. you deserve to.

- knives in my soul

i can not walk through this city without being reminded of you at every corner. the walls carry secrets between their cracks and the settling dust whispers heavily of a long-forgotten test of will. they call this spot the fountain of youth but i call it the fountain of truth because it is where you first looked at me like i was the only thing left in the world. you and i used to walk these streets while the rest of the world was asleep like we were invincible. invisible, escaping into our own world without a soul noticing our absence. the rooftop next door is where i saw you cry for the first time. the park down the street is where you helped me calm down when i begged for death that one summer night. the foundations of these buildings have witnessed the promises we made to each other. but the seasons have evolved. we walk under different skies. sometimes, i catch a hint of you in the breeze. but we are ghosts of our former pasts. walking forever empty streets searching for completeness and always missing each other by a few beats. darling, i have always loved you and i always will, but i think i would rather accept this defeat.

- shadows

you filled only the most
superficial parts of me
and this is why
i left

i have mastered the art
of completing all of your
sentences
but you won't even let me
finish mine

- love language

maybe you pulled him out of the fire
called yourself his savior
but in your awe
did you even notice
that with eyes as red as the devil himself
he brought kerosene in one pocket
and matchsticks in the other
so that he could continue to kindle the flames
and then leap back in with you trailing behind
because he knew
you were never one to give up on him

you see
people like this
have made a home out of hell
and they make it their principle to
spread the flames to whomever may
fall under their spell
so run the other direction
do not try to
liberate him from the burn
because he forgot how to feel the pain
long before you ever tried to save him from it

- in love with the way it burns pt. ii

she spent her nights praying for him
but he had other plans

    -    deceit

i do not desire the kind of love
that swallows me whole
and makes me forget everything
i ever was or am
i do not crave a love
that leaves me
gasping for air in the middle of the night
from exhilaration only to leave me
choking on my own tears at sunrise
i do not want to be a remembered prayer
and at the same time, a forgotten soul
a set of limbs for you to unfold
without knowing the heart within
so do not for one second believe that you
can get away with fulfilling the most
shallow parts of my existence
and think that it is enough

- my hands are full, but my heart is empty

## (w)holehearted

it is a new kind of hell when earthquakes of self-doubt begin to ripple through your core. the forests begin to look like trees again. hurricanes plow through your heart and destroy the self-esteem you worked so hard to build. your skin starts to look a little too earthy and hair falls out of your scalp faster than dead leaves during autumn. and then. then it is time to remember. remember the months you spent laying all the foundations for homes that the owners chose to finish without you. the weeks you built bridges between souls and were thrown promptly off the rails. the times you planted trees only to find dead leaves stuffed beneath your pillow. you were wide-eyed and young and innocent but all the sharp tongues stripped that away from you. perhaps if you built less bridges, lay down less bricks, and planted less trees, you could have saved yourself from this betrayal that blinds you more than you might already be to your own faults. your seemingly perfect landscape catches fire. you are left with nothing but ashes. the dirt of the remains crumbles in your fingertips. let the rage pass and then. then it is time to start over. you must till the soil. plant more seeds. cry in exhaustion. water the buds. plant flowers. pray. plant trees. pray. lay bricks. pray. a tornado comes. you slide halfway down the mountain. but still, you must water the plants. still you must climb. still you must build.

- the landscape of this earth is constantly changing. so it should come as no surprise that we, who are made of this same earth, are always changing too.

i want to go back to the days when things were simpler
when gray areas were cause for compromise
and right and wrong were easy to recognize
when fathers would provide and mothers would nurture
because that was the only definition of a family structure
when there was only one way to be religious
when being in love was nothing more than cooties and
mushy feelings while playing in a sandbox together
when we were too young to understand race
so all the different skin colors were just
part of the rainbow to our perfect sky
when death was something that happened to other people
and i could keep a dry eye
but crying was okay
when flowers were given only on anniversaries
when innocence was bliss
when simplicity was valued
and when kindness was my middle name

(w)holehearted

i want to go back to the days when pain was something
we didn't talk about
when gray areas only existed under your skin
and right and wrong weren't expanded to persecution
when i could pretend that everyone had a father
who would terrorize his children
when religion wasn't confusing
when being in love didn't tear up your insides
and make you want to die
when you were too young to understand race so you spent a party
scrubbing your black friend's arm, convinced that somehow
the color could wash off
when people we love didn't die tragic deaths every day
so crying was not for the weak-hearted
when flowers were not given at funerals
when ignorance really was bliss
and when we saw through the eyes of a child
up and coming into a world which was made to destroy him

- dissociation

i was never the kind of lover
that would deem the sky bluer
hear the birds sing louder
imagine that the summer breeze
seemed more perfect than usual
just because i was in love

it was quite the opposite actually
the world was still cruel
lightning would still strike unpredictably
there was still suffering all around me
but love
taught me to appreciate the good things

while they say love is blind
i journeyed through with eyes wide open
for while we live in an imperfect world
which will always remain that way
the moments i now cherish
were anything but that

- realistic

i'd been trying to write again for so long that i read every poem and listened to every song, yet the words never came until everything i had was gone, and my world became so empty and wrong.
pain and heartbreak wove their way onto paper and pen for the world to see. once upon a time, the ink ran dry, and of all things, tears came to rescue me.

- writer's block

awaken, arise
another day to live, a species to despise
dirty fingers play with dirty hair
lips cracked from dehydration left bare
tangled in a spiral of misery
ragged

actions, words
spewed out one in herds
empty promises fill my hollow stomach
as i listen to the ticking of the clock
and i wonder if our fate was real
destiny

on, it goes on
life stops for no one, games continue
everyone's living for themselves
selfish race we are indeed
peace found only when falsely achieved
happiness

heed, heed my words
there's a burning desire in my heart
to do this again, make it right
the way it should be, wait my turn
wait my time, until it's earned
patience

only, if only
a stranger, so lonely
make that vow, seal that bind
i'm waiting right here for you to find
chilled right down to the bone
alone

restless, endless
sleepless nights, tossing, turning, hoping
desperate for that one perfect moment
wishing for more than i could have dreamed
clinging on to that last hope in humanity

selfless

entranced, enchanted
surrounded by perfection
who knew such a thing existed?
you appear before my weary eyes
yours locked steadily on mine
silence

breathless, star-struck
i've waited so patiently, just my luck
for you i prayed, for you i dreamed
everything's coming together, it seems
just us two, hands intertwined
leaving the whole world behind
together

reality, duality
time heals all wounds, they say
i awaken from this beautiful nightmare
clinging to dreams
torn to shreds at the seams
broken

but waiting, i'll be waiting
an account far pre-written
something that can only be destined
someone real, someone true
peace encases my heart, comforting
warmth

nameless, faceless
one day i hope you leave me speechless
my loneliness will have to be tamed
and i may have yet to hear your name
but i know you're out there

    -   somewhere

my mother always told me to sleep on my right side
but it is only on my left that i can hear
the steady thump of my heart to remind me
how i am still alive
because in the midst of juggling the feeling of
wanting it all to end
and looking for a light at the end
of the tunnel
my insecurities eat me from toe up
all the way to my jugular
strip me of the very confidence i protect myself with
tell me that even god doesn't want me
and sometimes i believe these voices
how do you stop feeling nothing
when circumstances beg you to accept
that nothing is all you are?

- searching

in your arms
i both
healed through the comfort
and broke through the guilt
because being with you taught me
how to love my body
but hate my soul

- the cycle pt. iv

therapy
is there for you
to fight your demons
but what about when
you have to fight
your dad?

we fall for
charisma
every single time
something about
a personality so smooth
it sweeps us off our feet
and knocks all wind and common sense
out of us
but the thing about 'smooth'
is that it can be confused for 'slippery'
and before we know it
we've been seduced by a devil
in a beautiful disguise

- pretty boys with prettier promises

this knot of anxiety in my stomach
behind my ribs
in my chest
threatens to spill over into the new year
and i can't stop myself
from letting the poison seep through my veins
insecurities and all
crystal clear memories blur before my eyes or
maybe those are just tears that can think for themselves
which is better than i can say for most of us nowadays
and the darkness of this winter
and the pangs of this year
come to a close only to open
fresh wounds on another day
because beginnings are theoretical
wrapped up in pretty bows
to give us some inkling that things could
never get so bad again
but this world was never meant to be heaven
and our mistake is making it so
our mistake is running out of homes to build
in the things and people we think
can sustain the madness we are
but love
love won't always prevail
it will come damn near close
like a meteor just grazing the earth
and as survivors of this brutal time
we must prepare for more meteor showers
for more heartbreaks
for more disappointment
that maybe
maybe things won't get better

- but we will be

/ january 2017

"i promise i will always be here if you need me."
his shirt is soaked with my tears
and his voice is shaking
i can see the physical pain the heartbreak
is causing him
that i am causing him
yet he still chooses to comfort me
none of this is going as planned but i
can't stop falling apart
in his arms
"i have to be the one constant in your life,
don't i?"
and this is when my heart shatters

- breakups

summer comes to an end, and the future looks frightening from where i stand. i don't know what comes next and i fear what else this life might demand of me. this world is showing its true colors and god is slowly showing me the truth. i long for summer to never end for i don't know how much longer i can battle ignorance and youth. i turn twenty-two soon and i am bitter every year on that day, longing for my eighteenth year when i was among clearer days when i only saw black and white without any room for gray. now i am constantly wishing for my strength to remain, and i am hell-bent on making my demons pay for not letting my conscience stay. god has shown me how imperfect we are. i have found myself walking among stars, yet at the same time redemption seems so far. i miss the pure sweetness of faith and i long for its honeyed taste as i slowly climb back up this mountain i've created for myself. so i'm praying for a better fate with an open gate to truth and happier days. always thanking god for being so good to me along the way. *bismillah.*

(w)holehearted

*repairing*

face
your
feelings

if iron can remain soft
in the presence of fire
then why do our hearts
struggle to do the same?

- vulnerable

starting line
countdown begins
say your prayers
hundred-dollar shoes on your left
your hand-me-downs don't compare
left to right
toes on the line
no time for rebirth
did you even ask for this life?

the whistle blows and it's
ready, get set, go
as soon as you leave your mother's womb
stuck in this uncomfortable costume
but life was never meant to give you any wiggle room
the track is no different and it
will consume you

pass the hundred-meter line
pass a quarter of your life
the numbers keep adding up
you're out of breath and you wait for a sign
that you're
more than who you're behind
but you're
falling behind and
society begins to confine you
put you in boxes you never
asked to be divided into
hierarchies
income
color of your skin
the width of your waist
the monsters within
survival of the fittest
and you were never the most fit
bit by bit
the other runners pass you
society teaches you to submit
you learn to admit that

you're not special
you were never meant to stand out
or be influential

and the longer you run
the more you realize that you are just
a number on the track
your weight bracket
your height
the width of your thighs
whitewashed beady eyes carefully scrutinize
every inch of you 'til you
cease to recognize
who you were at the starting line
this world is a race
and those who are weak will be left behind
forget about ever crossing that anticipated finish line

the timer ticks and your feet slip
as exhaustion sets in from your journey's quips
the thirst for recognition
the sun in your eyes
maybe the world decided
you were destined to remain blind
and that was your fate
your final demise
to watch yourself run as fast
as you possibly could
but never be as good
watch your friends
your family
your loved ones
people richer than you
people better than you
people smarter than you
people faster than you
there will always be people faster than you
there will always be people who finish before you
and playing catch up is a death sentence
long overdue

some of us never make it to the end
this race
this world
is slowly breaking us
depriving us of
water and life
where it is not enough anymore
to claim that you tried
the system is designed to
never let us reach the end
let alone be first
but instead fills us with
just the right amount of hot air
'til we burst
teaches us to confuse lust for love
contentment for material things
and happiness for smiles
but who are we kidding?
we are failing
and continuing to run was
never worthwhile
from the start
we were losing this race
trying to save face
it's about time we
came to terms with the fact that
we have a place
in this world
and it is not at the top
but if you've spent your life running this long
what makes you think
you would ever be able to stop?

- dehydration

## (w)holehearted

as the melancholy dissipates
the ink wells of my veins run dry
i can't remember the last time i felt
the need to write
these last few weeks
breathing hasn't been a chore
the panic has all but exited my blood
it no longer feels like it is a part of me
but isn't it intriguing how sadness works
we cling on to it for so long
that we forget who we are when it vanishes
the pens of my soul haven't been lifted in
what feels like ages
i don't remember who i am
without my words
which i suppose also means
i've forgotten who i am
without my pain

- writer's block ii

how can one live
in a world of sunrises
and deny the existence
of god?

## (w)holehearted

*after huda bint adnan*

there are so many questions i want to ask
like how much did it hurt
when you relived your sins in these pages
and if the walls in your room
ever spoke the truth
if the bruises and cuts on your arms
ever healed
and if after loving him so much
did you lose your ability to feel?
but i need not ask
i need not dig
because at the end of the day i
am recovering from devils making a similar
meal out of my blood
and your silence is not needed
for me to know
the healing will take
a while

- to my favorite poet

i ache to think about
all the pieces of myself
i missed out on
simply because i was too afraid
to put them back together

you began as
nothing
but a seed
in the womb
of your mother
who bloomed
allowing you
to enter this world

what makes you believe
you owe her anything
less
than the fruits
of her labor?

- roots | grounded

show me your wounds
open your heart up deep as you can go
i was always told i could be a doctor but
i am made to help you heal yourself
give me your tears, your pain, your insecurities
and i will keep it all safe for you
file you into a cabinet at the end of the night
and tuck your memories into bed and out of sight
until the next week
when it is time to open you up again
i will show you how to breathe by yourself
remind you that only you can complete yourself
i am not and never will be your superhero
merely a leg to your table
the fluff to your pillow
teach you how to swim so you can backstroke
the way through your own tears
you are not just a checklist
or a specimen under my lens
but i will serve as a means to an end
a bridge to the light, the water to your flowers
so seek my help, but you will find only you
as for me, i'll be a distant memory
bags under eyes, but forever satisfied
at my love for giving someone
another way to view life

- an ode to social workers

i've felt
so much
of nothing
for
so much
of my life
that
to wake up
with anxiety
hollowing out
my stomach
has become
a relief

- empty

your faith is divine
and must be carried in a vessel
as worthy as itself
do not place it in the hands of mortality
a container so fragile
it will continue to shatter your certainty
in everything you believe is pure

- on reliance of community for one's spirituality; for souls who can't seem to find that niche these days

notice how all the birds of the world
convene together at
*fajr* and *maghrib*
notice how even the animals
were made to remember god
at the rising and setting
of the sun

- prayer is a gift to creation

the first boy you love
will teach you
that you in all your young years
have no inkling of the concept of love
that you are not remotely prepared
for the worst is yet to come
the second will write you poems
and evoke words in you
that you would never dare say aloud
and he will break you
you will want to die and you will believe
that nothing else could possibly hurt
worse than this
and you will be right because
the third
won't be the one for you but
he will love you more than you love him
he will have a hard time letting you go
and the pain in his eyes will remind you
of all the times you cried over him
and all the ones before
this will show you
who is truly deserving of you
and the damage that's left scars
too deep to fill with third and fourth chances
will teach you to spend time catering to them
before opening yourself up once more

- at the end, the only thing that's left is you

take the words they cut you with
turn the blood into ink
write with it
watch the poetry heal the wounds

- your tongue still isn't as sharp as my mind

i found god in salty seas and the ocean breeze, and remembering his glory put me at ease. curling white sand beneath my toes while sitting on the beach composing prose. inhaling the scent of wildflowers in the air with fireflies landing in my hair. i found god in airplanes while soaring thirty thousand feet above, and it was through awe of his creations that i immersed myself in his love.

- finding god

i. the world underestimates the importance of fathers. i can bring thousands of stories of bad choices to the table as evidence to beg the men listening never to abandon their daughters.

ii. i was sitting in chemistry class in tenth grade learning about ions and thinking about the first boy i had ever fallen in love with. when, with what felt like the rupture of a black hole in my gut, as if to punish me, my body caved into a deep sadness, reminding me of what i had been missing all my life. father. dad. warmth. strong arms. protection. a different kind of love. male love. the first man i was ever supposed to love. i had tried to find him in the presence and scent and embraces of other men, family members, and lovers. but it was never quite the same.

iii. women like me will admit to some type of void in their lives. absent father. distant father. abusive father. it doesn't matter. some voids are worse than others. all of us develop fissures in our hearts that grow with each passing year. until we fill it with rocks and other all-consuming relationships that settle in the pits of our stomachs and refuse to leave.

iv. i am not sure what gets us through. we either learn to detach so thoroughly that we convince ourselves we don't need relationships at all. or we fall so hard for others, so deeply, that we forget who we are without them to remind us. we are daughters of two extremes. children of broken homes. victims of men who thought about themselves before they thought about the consequences.

v. we are the consequences.

- (w)holehearted

rain washes away all the dirt of a clouded mind
rain brings out the poetry within
اللّهُمَّ صَيِّباً نافِعاً

(w)holehearted

we were sitting in a wide open hall
rain pattering on the roof
above our heads
i was wearing a pink dress
you were on the phone
in your usual black
it was deserted
and i couldn't take my eyes
off of you

i couldn't resist so
i leaned over and kissed
your forehead
you grabbed my hand
still on the phone
but your eyes
filled with wonder
like a child with all his dreams
coming true

it has been
so many years
since i left
but that look
in your eyes
hasn't

- the eyes say more than the lips ever can

i have watched everyone
choose you over me:
the love of my life
the ones i called family
sometimes even myself
so please forgive me for finally
putting myself first
because the last straw
was when you left me in the dust too

- i am sorry for my resentment
  but after all, i am only human

all the men
i ever encountered
never
let me
speak

this
is why i
began
to write

    -   avenues

describing yourself
as an emotional person
is just another way of
saying you are human

- a response to "you are too emotional"

## (w)holehearted

heights and flights never deter me
from eagerly looking through small glass windows
rays of light
stretched beyond the eye can see
with armies of clouds to assist this beauty
orange hues, cotton candy skies
these are the colors before my very eyes
god puts in front of me to witness his sun
rise every morning
set every night
to think that he could take this away
in the blink of an eye
but traveling by air is such a beautiful thing
the daytime highlights all of god's creations
the night shows you all of man's
rolling hills, then twinkling lights
i am forever grateful
for every opportunity to look down from up high
but no matter how much god shows me
a fraction of what it's like to see the world
from his eyes
i will never get my fill
of the beauty of these skies

- airplanes

five reasons (intersectional) feminism exists:

i. when men say that women are too emotional
i am starting to realize that's a good thing
because as a woman, i'd much rather be able to experience
the full spectrum of the human emotion instead of
the singular phenomenon of toxic masculinity
or call it anger
call it abuse
call it burying your daughters
call it starting world wars
how do men
expect god to be compassionate towards them
when they consider compassion a weakness?
i am learning
that our ability to think with passion actually makes us stable
and that it is the furthest thing from a weakness
i have learned
that fighting for power is a game you play when you are choking
from swallowing too much of it in the first place.

ii. the plumber is supposed to fix our sink sometime on monday
between 8 am and 12 pm
i take off work that morning and tell my boss i will be there at 12:30
he strolls up to our door at 11:45
and when i ask him how long the job will take
he has the audacity to call me bossy.

iii. i've spent these days rebuilding my body
after ripping it apart with the words
of careless aunties and paper cuts from teen vogue
and the sharp waists of all the white women
bestowed upon my self esteem
i am teaching myself to be beautiful again
to love all the hairs that harvested themselves on my skin
to refrain from dissecting my eyebrows
like white men have done to my culture
to take pride in the bridge of my nose and
my thick eyelashes and
bask in all my melanin's glory.

iv. the liver is the only organ in the human body
that can regenerate itself; take note, the heart can not
so when we tell our women to move on
after a rape, after an assault, after the man who cheated on her,
after the madman, the psychopath man,
the "men will be men" kind of man
we assume that moving on without fractures and battle scars
from wars that men waged on us
is even a possibility
i think god
knew what he was doing
when he created woman from a man's rib
and then made the rest of mankind emerge from between her thighs
to prove that we may look fragile
but we are able to survive the process
of birthing sons that will grow up to think
it is their god given right to make women scream in pain
and i thank god
that even though our hearts can't regenerate themselves
the spark that these injustices create within us
is enough to set them on fire.

v. they call us "pearls," "flowers," say we are fragile and sweet
associate these words with femininity
as if there is only one way to be woman
call us delicate and say that we must be "preserved"
but then pick out our petals one by one
savoring the pain, cracking the pearls in half
and reminding us that even our femininity
belongs to them alone
then they wonder why we protest
why we breathe fire
why we have learned to take control of a pain
that was never meant to be ours in the first place
they call us flowers
but everything they say makes us soft
makes us a woman
has been stolen from us
and what you see now is
what is left.

how can a species
created with so much love
be capable of such hatred?

- human

(w)holehearted

a five-minute conversation
and a little bit of insight
that's how you can distinguish
the most incredible humans on earth
from the rest

tongues of honey
a presence drowning in *noor*
devoted soldiers through and through
emitting an aura of
complete tranquility
and *tawakkul*

these are the ones
who were destined for heaven
before birth
and all you can wish
is for them to take you too

- people of *allah*

the love
doesn't exist yet
but
every smile
every gesture
every kind word
is slowly bringing
me
home

    - falling

saved and
protected me
loved and
guided me
gave me hope
set me free
how then
can i not be
grateful for
your mercy?

- *ar-rashid*

my first love
used to
write me poems
tell me he wanted to marry me
and then fly off into the wind
where i wouldn't
hear from him for months

my second love
was the kind that consumed you whole
until where i began and
where he ended
was wrapped in a tangled web
of limbs and
circumstances
beyond our control

the third
is a perfect balance
between god and earth
milk and honey
and everything pure in this world
and i know
that i don't
deserve
him

- they say the third time is a charm

(w)holehearted

i'm convinced that if i
hadn't spent so much
time persuading myself
that i wasn't good enough
i would have had more
time to engage in habits
that would make me
better

- thought restructuring

i keep finding white hairs
all over my clothes and on my towels
and it took me a painfully long time
to realize they belonged to my mother
my mother wears her mane
of salt-and-pepper hair like a crown
unapologetic of her age with a confidence
one could only muster the courage to dream of
meanwhile the auntie at my job with two kids
says that i shouldn't ask people their age
that it isn't polite
but tell me
how can i force myself to be ashamed
of something that is just a part of life
and why have we become slaves to numbers
weight, age, even shoe sizes have become
something to be embarrassed about
numbers are simply numbers and my mother
a powerhouse with fifty-three years on her
and five feet two inches of pride
proves that so well

- the numbers game

i will never ask you to wake me up for *fajr*
what i will ask is
if you know how to wake up for *fajr*
without me

- to my future husband

a chorus of *ameens* echoing throughout the halls
the caress of fingers making handprint marks
on lined carpets
gentle thuds of hundreds of knees falling
to the floor in prostration
earth-shattering *surahs* recited in perfect harmony
the whispers of private prayers
asking
longing from their lord
our everyday hymns
simple
and so very soothing

- *masjid* melodies

i. *ramadan* 30 1437, 8:18 p.m.
i am mesmerized
by the last sunset of *ramadan*
the sky is on fire
hues of orange and pink splattered
across the atmosphere
as if *ramadan* wanted to leave
with an impression
i desperately count the seconds
not waiting for *iftar*
like the twenty-nine days before
but tears welling up
as i mourn the month which
spared my soul but took
so many others'
as it departed

ii. *shawwal* 1, 1437, 9:09 p.m.
hopeful
at the sight of the sliver
of the new *shawwal* moon
peeping through the window
on my entire bus ride home
as if to reassure me
that with every fiery sunset ending
comes a new birth
and a new beginning

- post-*ramadan* blues

god always told me
to wait for something better
and i knew he was right
when i found you

## (w)holehearted

there is a melancholic sweetness in the air when you experience short-lived moments of pure emotion after feeling nothing for so long. the exhilaration, the adrenaline, the love you briefly feel for a world which has shoved you into boxes you were never meant to fit into. my shoulders hunch from burdens i was never meant to carry but tonight, i let it all go. jumping from pillar to pillar makes my heart race in ways i forgot it had the capability of doing so. my feet cave inwards as the years give up on them ever being walkable. and normal. but then again, nothing about me has ever been normal and i am learning to be okay with this. my skin gleams with sweat and pockmarks and scars and i have no desire to disguise them. my veins are alight with anticipation. my eyes widen in awe as i look around and i realize how mankind has surely carved its mark on this world in the strangest of ways but i know god gave us the ability to do so. so i will appreciate what god presented to me. i will teach myself to feel again. to love again. to break again and get back up again. to roam this world and love every flower, every tree, every soul. myself. me.

- journey

in the chilling whispers of the night
when thoughts begin to race and take flight
as i listen to my shallow breathing
and the thump of my heart's rhythmic beating
is when emotions pour out one by one
i try to escape them; i try to run
anxiety creeps in like roots of a tree
suffocating in darkness deeper than i can see
blinded by a despicable hatred
as i watch those dear to me become alienated
the walls inside me i so carefully rebuilt
have crumbled away with tears of guilt
it's not fair but it's no use
i've repeatedly broken my own truce
what happened to me? what have i become?
to which downfall did i succumb?
i turn every corner to face an obstruction
while life as i know it spirals into destruction
i chain my wrists to planks of shame
only to break the metal and restart the game
but alas, peace overcomes my soul
for the prewritten will always remain in the scroll
and *allah* afflicts his believers with trials
to see who can attain *jannah* with winning smiles
in this bittersweet solitude of mine
i find neither death, nor a lifeline
only acceptance of a healing by time
a soothing remedy of prose and rhyme
so vanquish all the worries and sorrows
life is too beautiful to beg for a different tomorrow
i refuse to let my fears win over me
and steal what little time i'm guaranteed
the youth in my body will fade away with age
but i'll let the youth in my soul forever remain
and i'll smile at the blessings of the unknown
time ticks away as i watch the sun rise alone

- bittersweet solitude

you reek of this world
but i
have always longed
for the fragrance of heaven

- *ahl al-jannah*

think of the events in your life and the people you meet like various features of the earth. some will come into your life like the sky. sometimes they will change colors from a calming blue to a smooth black, but you will always be able to look up and know that they are there. then there will be people who will bestow themselves upon you like a rainfall. they will cleanse you and plant flowers in your esophagus, under your tongue, and along your ribs, allowing you to bloom in places you never dreamed of. and then there will be those who come into your life like a raging river. they will sweep you off your feet and never allow you to look back. you will carve paths with them through mountains and valleys and eventually learn that you can take control of the current. that you can create your own journey. so you will learn to branch off. and then, there will be some who just watch. those are the hurricanes waiting to form but you must always remember that you are the eye of the storm. that you have more control of your seasons than they will ever dream of. you will learn to strive for more sky in your life, but you must remember that the weather is always unpredictable. that wind currents may blow themselves your way and all you can do is keep pushing them through you until they reach the other side. after years of hurricanes and sunsets and disappointments, you will teach yourself how to manipulate the currents just enough to where the destruction and rainfall they unleash upon you will create the majestic landscape that you are today. and you will thank the raging river. you will thank the sky. you will even thank the hurricanes. because the landscape that will be you is jagged and unique and imperfectly beautiful. as it is meant to be. as you were always meant to be.

- storms and sunshine are equally good for (your) growth

i often wonder
when i die
how i will be remembered
will i be known
as the girl who took risks
or the woman who couldn't stand firmly
by what she believed in?
will i be known
as the daughter of a hardworking single mother
or as the five foot two, unapologetic woman
no matter the consequences?
will i be called
kind before pretty
brave before sweet
a humanitarian before an influencer
or the other way around?
will i be missed
i wonder
will the world mourn me
i wonder
and will god welcome me home
praising me with these same words?

- legacy

my father told me a few years ago that i was going to hell for testifying against him in court for the divorce case. i walked out of the therapist's room crying, convinced that there would be no turning back from this. that any minimal progress on making things civil was a lost cause. today, it is the seventh day of *ramadan*, and we are eating pizza at a restaurant we stumbled upon, watching the sun set. i tell him about the guy i am seeing and he asks three questions before the conversation continues moving. sometimes i wonder if he is just burying his former self because he knows we are adults now and don't tolerate any outrageous behavior, or if he has actually changed and eliminated some of his tendencies. i wonder how many brown muslim girls could tell their fathers about getting engaged in the near future and have them be happy about it, but from a distance, without any more to say. how was i to realize walking out of that therapist's office five years ago that it would be this way now. how different this is from all the fears i envisioned would come to life. how drastically has my own perception shifted to where i don't need him to say 'i love you' anymore. i see it in the way he pays for us and in how he comes down to visit us every few months. in the "happy mother's day" texts he sends, reminding us to respect and care for mamma. as a young girl i searched for verbal validation of my existence, but i am learning that love comes in different forms, and is shown in different ways. and that our parents aren't perfect. but they are human. and just like we don't have it all figured out, they really don't either.

- meeting #17

i hear my mother
lament to god habitually
invoking his name at all hours
her relationship with him
goes beyond five conversations a day
she prays for us in every breath
and stands at 4 a.m.
on her now gracefully aging feet
while the rest of us sleep
begging him to protect us from things
we don't even have the words for
and begs him to protect
our children to come
this is the grace of a mother
who is overflowing with so much love
she remembers to pray for people
who have yet to exist

- if i could be half the woman she is

*our lord, perfect for us our light and forgive us.
indeed, you are over all things, competent.*

*qur'an 66:8*

*oh allah! i seek refuge in you from grief and sadness, from weakness and from laziness, from miserliness and from cowardice, from being overcome by debt and from being overpowered by men (and others).*

*sahih bukhari 7:158*

acknowledgements and thanks:

where to begin?

all praises to allah (swt) for allowing me to accomplish a dream i have had for years. for giving me the drive to follow through with what i started. and for gifting me with the love of writing poetry, as it aligns with the traditions and spirit of islam.

to my mother, who doesn't always approve of my poetry but supports me anyway. mothers are truly special and although my tributes to them in this book aren't worth a fraction of what they give us, i hope they resonate with all who read them.

to aisha, who was the original poet, artist, and talented one in the family, for secretly being my cheerleader and enduring all the comments about being known as "sara's sister."

to usama, for being my inspiration. your ability to love speaks volumes and languages that are beyond the spine of these pages.

to amina, my best friend and main hypewoman, i can't begin to describe your contributions to this, but your stunning cover art would be a great place to start.

to huda, (a talented self-published poet herself) for unknowingly inspiring me to start sharing my poetry publicly and for the painstaking hours you put in to edit this book for me.

to saad, humna, and faraaz, for making me laugh and blush with your (slightly exaggerated) promotions of my work. it is always humbling to have friends who are even more excited about your accomplishments than you are.

to fatima, muhajir, batool, mariam, sehrish, hiba, kainat, maryam, yushra, farhan, sanam, and probably countless more names i am leaving out, for your love, encouragement, advice, coaching, and collaboration.

to my brother, may time and kindness heal all our wounds.

to my father, for mastering the art of stepping back and letting go. for making the effort to stay in my life, even when there was a time i didn't want you there.

thank you always.

CPSIA information can be obtained
at www.ICGtesting.com
Printed in the USA
LVHW021338090521
686914LV00013B/1508